WILL&KATE

A ROYAL FAMILY

Publisher and Creative Director: Nick Wells
Project Editor: Polly Prior
Picture Research: Josie Mitchell
Art Director: Mike Spender
Digital Design and Production: Chris Herbert

Special thanks to: Cat Taylor, Stephen Feather, Dawn Laker, Laura Bulbeck and Karen Fitzpatrick

ISBN 978-1-78361-613-8

Manufactured in China

1 3 5 7 9 10 8 6 4 2

WILL&KATE

A ROYAL FAMILY

ALICE HUDSON

FOREWORD BY JOE LITTLE, *MAJESTY* MAGAZINE

**FLAME TREE
PUBLISHING**

Contents

Foreword

When, on 16 November 2010, it was finally announced that HRH Prince William of Wales and Miss Catherine Middleton were to marry, the next edition of *Majesty* magazine was about to go to press. For the first – and probably only – time in my career I had to instruct the printers to 'hold the front page' so that I could run with a picture of the newly-engaged couple.

I soon started to receive telephone calls from media organisations around the globe, eager for a comment on the breaking news. At the time, neither I nor my fellow royal correspondents could have guessed what an impact the William and Kate love story would have on people, not just in the following days and weeks but for the next six months too; we had never experienced anything quite like it. And yet why wouldn't the world be interested in a young, attractive couple, particularly when he'd topped the 'Most Eligible Bachelor' lists for so long?

It therefore came as no surprise to be told that an estimated two billion people had watched the 'Wedding of the Century' on television or by other means. But the fascination with the Duke and Duchess of Cambridge continues: their tour of Canada last summer was an incredible success, they were feted by Hollywood A-listers during a working weekend in Los Angeles and back at home every time an item from Kate's high-street wardrobe is identified by fashionistas it sells out immediately.

William and Kate must take much of the credit for the soaring popularity of the British royal family right now. Their relaxed, no-nonsense approach to the way they live their lives has won them many new admirers, who until now had regarded the House of Windsor as posh, privileged and past its sell-by date.

Joe Little

Managing Editor, Majesty Magazine

A Fairy-Tale Romance

Second in line to the British throne by blue-blooded birthright, HRH Prince William has long been the subject of girlish princess fantasies the world over. On 29 April 2011, one of the world's most eligible bachelors finally became officially spoken for. After a nine-year courtship, Catherine (Kate) Middleton – stylish, accessibly beautiful and middle class – married her prince. Catherine, the Duchess of Cambridge as she is now known, will one day become Queen Consort, providing hubby William takes the throne.

The first 'commoner' with no aristocratic titles to marry into the British Royal Family in 350 years, Kate's fairy-tale wedding was a global news event of epic proportions – attracting two billion viewers worldwide. Across the UK, flag-bearing masses whipped themselves into a wedding frenzy, while an adoring public in the hundreds of thousands happily thronged London's streets. It was a day to go down in history. Will and Kate's lives have since been closely followed by the media and public, especially as the happy couple became parents for the first, and then the second, time.

A Popular Pair

William and Kate have long enjoyed the approval of each other's families. The public seem to think it a good match

'He'll be thrilled if she's a hit with the public. He's not like his father in this respect. Nothing would please him more than to find people surging past him so that they can get a good look at Kate.'

A Palace aide

'We all think he is wonderful
and we are extremely fond of him.
They make a lovely couple, they
are great fun to be with, and we've
had a lot of laughs together.'

Michael Middleton, speaking following

the engagement announcement

'There's been a lot of speculation about every single girl I'm with and it actually does quite irritate me after a while, more so because it's a complete pain for the girls.'

Prince William

too, judging by the thousands of wedding celebrations – complete with bunting – held worldwide in their honour. Glamorous, yet down to earth, pretty, yet serious-minded, Kate is an excellent match for William – a self-described 'country boy at heart'.

Kate's modest style, natural poise, easy charm, intelligence and, above all, unrelenting discretion, are named by royal watchers as traits making her an appropriate choice for a future king. Their relationship has helped revive positive press for a monarchy marred by scandal; rejuvenating a family long considered overly stuffy and out of touch. Young, glamorous, rich and royal – and with two gorgeous young children – Will and Kate appear to have it all.

Media Spotlight

Prince William grew up in the media spotlight. While naturally shy, he became accustomed to the attention that was a given for members of 'The Firm'. During his formative years, the sensitive youngster was a first-hand witness to his mother's harassment by paparazzi, as she became increasingly hounded, right up until the night of her tragic death. The media would remain a source of extreme tension for William for many years to come. To this day, he and Kate fiercely guard their privacy, and even more so, that of their children.

A Mother's Influence

Prince William was 15 years old when his mother died in a Paris car crash on 31 August 1997. The speeding car she was a passenger in was being pursued by paparazzi at the time of the crash. William had always enjoyed a particularly close bond with his mother. He inherited more than her blond locks and bashful, endearing smile – the pair sharing similar sensitive, charitable and down-to-earth natures.

Remembered as a devoted mother who made sure both William and his younger brother, Harry, were exposed to a wider range of experiences than is usual for royal children, Diana famously took them on trips to Walt Disney World and McDonalds. She indulged them with video games while broadening their minds by taking them to AIDS clinics and homeless shelters. Very 'hands on', lacking the traditional stuffiness common in the Royal Family, Diana rarely deferred to her husband, or his family, when it came to decisions such as where to send her boys to school. The story about when William, aged seven, said he wanted to be a policeman when he grew up so he could 'protect' his mother is a touching one. It was little brother Harry who allegedly instantly responded: 'Oh, no you can't. You've got to be King.'

Education of a Prince

William kicked off his education, aged three, at Mrs Mynor's Nursery School in West London. While there, he performed in a nursery school play, even singing a musical solo. Aged

'Losing a close family member is one of the hardest experiences that anyone can endure. Never being able to say the word "mummy" again in your life sounds like a small thing. However, for many, including me, it's now really just a word – hollow and evoking memories.'

William speaking out for the first time about his mother's death

four, he graduated to the equally posh Wetherby School. Both Charles and Diana took part in parents' races at the annual sports day. William himself showed an early passion for sports. A natural in the water, aged seven he won a trophy for 'best swimming style'.

'I like to be in control of my life because I have so many people around me, I can get pulled in one direction, and then the other… I could actually lose my identity.'

Prince William

In 1990, William began the first of five years at Ludgrove School in Berkshire, where he kept swimming while taking up football, basketball, clay pigeon shooting and cross-country running. William broke royal tradition to attend Eton College. There, he studied geography, biology and art history. Always extremely popular among his peers, the talented and intelligent teen captained his house football team, took up water polo and achieved 12 GCSEs and three A Levels. Before university, he took a 'gap' year. During this time, he taught children in Chile, took part in British Army training exercises in Belize, worked on British dairy farms and visited countries in Africa.

'William is a country boy. His mother used to ring me up and say, "William is like a caged lion in London. Can he come and spend the day with your family?"'

Lady Annabel Goldsmith

'He loves informality and wants to be treated like everyone else. He once asked a teacher [at Eton] who addressed him as Prince William to "drop the name"'.

A source at Eton

There's Something About The Girl

Catherine Elizabeth Middleton was born on 9 January 1982. She grew up with an ordinary name in an ordinary village, Bucklebury, in Berkshire, England. Catherine's parents had no aristocratic links – descended from coal miners and clergymen. Her father, a former flight dispatcher, had met her mother, an air hostess, while the pair were working for British Airways. By the time Kate was five, her parents had left their frequent flyer days behind them to set up a successful party supplies business – it is now a £30 million operation.

So while 'Kate', as she was known, was no blue blood, she, sister Pippa and brother James certainly enjoyed a very comfortable upbringing. One popular story told by locals in Kate's local area tells of the pleasure her grandmother, who died in 2006, would have got from Kate's wedding. A coal miner's granddaughter, she was allegedly known as 'Lady Dorothy' by some relatives, as she was fanatical about keeping up appearances and 'wanted to be the top brick in the chimney'.

School Days

Catherine began her education abroad, at an English language nursery school in Jordan, where her parents were temporarily based while still employed by British Airways.

'Those people who were so recently sneering at her background, and nicknaming her "Waity Katie", will soon be lost in admiration of her poise and professionalism.'

Historian Andrew Roberts

Upon their return to Berkshire, Kate was enrolled at co-educational preparatory school St Andrew's, in the nearby village of Pangbourne, which set her parents back a cool £13,000 a year in fees. Determined to offer their daughter the best possible education, they then sent her on to Downe House in Cold Ash, near Newbury, where fees are around £10,000 per term. Kate was a day girl at the girls' boarding school, putting her in the minority. By all accounts, she did not enjoy the place and, after just two terms, she upped and left for Marlborough College.

> *'I was quite nervous about meeting William's father but he was very, very welcoming and very friendly.'*
>
> *Kate Middleton*

According to some media reports, Kate was bullied relentlessly at Downe by cliquey, bitchy girls, who saw her as too 'skinny', 'nice' and 'meek'. Kate's former headmistress at Downe was forced to insist there was no 'serious' harassment, although she admitted the 'catty' atmosphere and classroom pranks could have left young Kate feeling 'like a fish out of water'. At Marlborough, Kate put any previous troubles behind her, becoming a successful all-rounder and school prefect.

> *'Kate is straightforward, nice, composed, feminine and very English. Discreet and quiet, but with a strong sense of herself. She's a classy girl.'*
>
> *Jewellery designer Claudia Bradby, who worked with Kate when she was employed as a part-time junior buyer for Jigsaw*

'She's stunning. She's really, really good-looking. She just seemed to be very natural. She had that natural beauty. She still does, but at that time, we didn't know who she was and she did stand out, yeah.'

Sophie Butler, Kate's hairdresser while she was studying

A popular rumour says Kate entertained royal fantasies while at boarding school, pinning a poster of William – the heartthrob prince – on her wall. While Kate rarely adds to media speculation, this is one story she has laughingly denied. 'He wishes,' she said at the official engagement interview. 'I had the Levi's guy on my wall, not a picture of William.'

'He's lucky to be going out with me.'

Kate Middleton

Interests and Strengths

As well as being intelligent and studious, Kate has always been a natural sportswoman. As a child, she relished ski holidays with the family, while competing successfully in a wide range of school sports, including athletics, tennis, field hockey and netball. As if that was not enough, Kate, a former Girl Guide, also excelled culturally. She once played Eliza Doolittle in *My Fair Lady*, learned ballet and tap dancing and was a skilled flautist and singer. According to *Hello* magazine, school pals called her 'a kind-hearted and sensible soul who rarely caused upset among her peers'.

'When I first met Kate,

I knew there was something

very special about her.

I knew there was possibly

something that I wanted

to explore there.'

Prince William

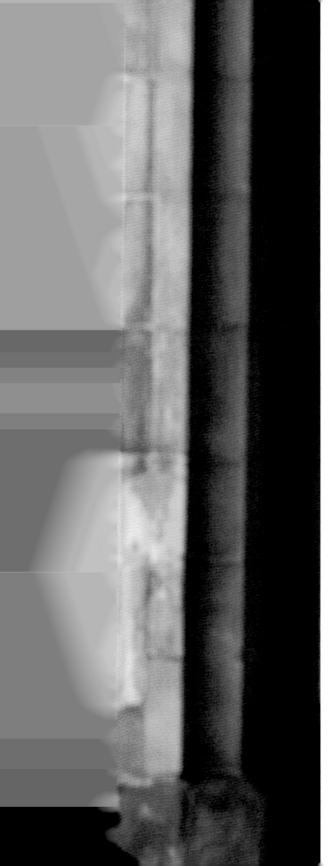

University Romance

Brian Lang, the ex-principal of St Andrews University, said at the graduation of William and Kate in June 2005, 'You'll have made lifelong friends. Not only that, and I say this every year to every group of the new St Andrews graduates: you may have met your husband or wife. Our title as the top matchmaking university in Britain is at stake.' Truer words could not have been spoken for two particular people.

St Andrews

Fresh from his adventurous gap year, William enrolled at the University of St Andrews in Fife, Scotland. The news a Royal would be among the freshers reportedly caused an influx of last-minute applications to study there – the majority from female students. Kate Middleton can hardly have imagined the huge consequences her own decision to study at St Andrews would have. Placed in the same school residence as HRH, Kate has since admitted she 'went red and sort of scuttled off' the first time she was introduced to her famous classmate. However, the pair soon became good buddies. As William has described it, they enjoyed a 'good giggle and lots of fun' together at Saint Salvator's, known as 'Sallies' – the hall of residence they both bunked down in.

First Meeting

Exactly when the two hooked up is not publicly known, but William has claimed when they moved in together at the beginning of their second year, it was purely as friends and flatmates. 'We were friends for over a year first and it just sort of blossomed from then on,' the Prince has explained. He has called their friendship a 'good foundation' for the relationship. 'I do generally believe now that being friends with one another is a massive advantage.'

One popular theory is that William was awakened to Kate's charms when he saw her strutting down the catwalk for a student fashion show, DON'T WALK, in 2002, wearing a sheer (now famous) dress that left little to the imagination. Once he had his eye firmly on the prize, Will went all out to woo his girl.

'When I was trying to impress Kate, I was trying to cook these amazing fancy dinners and all that would happen was I'd burn something. Or something would overspill, or something would catch on fire,' he recounted later. 'She'd be sitting in the background just trying to help and basically taking control of the whole situation.'

Just Good Friends

While William has admitted his housemate romance with Kate at first bemused their friends, it was hardly surprising the two found common ground, despite her middle-class upbringing and his royal one. Their relationship has always been based on friendship and shared interests. Both began university majoring in art history, although William later changed his major to geography, a decision Kate is said to have advised him on. Both did well at their studies and were popular with their peers, although they also loved a good night out dancing, balanced with enough studying to ensure they made their respective families proud. William and Kate both earned Master of Arts degrees, with upper second-class honours; William in geography and Kate in History of Art.

While at university, Prince William represented the Scottish national universities' water polo team at the Celtic Nations tournament in 2004, while Kate kept her love of sports up too, running and rowing among her favourites. 'We had a really good laugh, and then, things happened,' was how Prince William would later explain the natural progression of the relationship.

'My guiding principles in life are to be honest, genuine, thoughtful and caring.'
Prince William

'I first met her at Peter and Autumn's wedding and it was in amongst a lot of other guests and she was very friendly.'

Kate on meeting the Queen.

Media Scrutiny

Any girlfriend of William's was always going to come under intense media scrutiny. So while rumours of the relationship circulated for years, the two held off confirming they were a couple until 2004, following a March ski trip in Klosters, Switzerland, with Harry and Charles, where they were pictured together looking cosy. The couple were protected from press intrusion to a large degree at St Andrews due to a 'gentleman's agreement' between newspaper editors and the Royal household. Will was known as 'Steve' by other students to avoid any journalists overhearing and realizing his identity.

'She's got a really naughty sense of humour which helps me, as I've got a really dirty sense of humour.'

William on Kate

The Prince desperately wanted to protect his girlfriend from the tabloid scrutiny that had plagued his mother. While not wanting to shirk his own royal duties and responsibilities, Prince William has always maintained that: 'What I do with my private life is really between me and myself, basically.'

'They could go down
to the beach, they could
come for drinks here.
They could just behave
like a normal couple'.

Justin Hughes, ex-owner of

MA BELLS, *a St Andrews*

haunt of the couple

Finding Themselves

While at St Andrews, the media had kept their promise not to hound the couple. Once Kate and Will graduated and headed to the capital, stress-free nights out with friends became nearly impossible, while pressure began to mount from all sides. Intense speculation about a forthcoming engagement grew to the extent where one hasty company even produced a range of celebratory cups and plates. There would be no rushing the couple, however. Painfully aware of the outcome of his parents' marriage – which eventually ended in divorce in 1996 – William was determined history would not repeat itself. His desire to protect Kate was coupled with a determination to concentrate on his military career and a refusal to be pushed into marriage. Tough times were ahead for the high-profile lovers.

Careers

William wasted no time throwing himself into military training. He began his career as an officer cadet at the Royal Military Academy at Sandhurst, joining younger brother Harry. After completing his training in December 2006, he received a commission as 2nd Lieutenant in the Blues and Royals regiment before becoming a troop commander in an armed reconnaissance unit. 'The last thing I want is to be mollycoddled or be wrapped up in cotton wool', he publicly declared. After

completing attachments with the Royal Air Force and Royal Navy, William set his sights on becoming an RAF Search and Rescue pilot, a position he still holds today. William's military posts provided periods of relief from the media spotlight; however, Kate, in London, struggled to lead anything like a normal twenty-something life. She secured a job as an accessories buyer for retailer Jigsaw and later joined the family party supplies business as a photographer. It seemed to the world she was a princess-in-waiting, leading to the media nickname, 'Waity Katie'.

Media Invasion

Both private people by nature, the young couple grew increasingly frustrated with the constant throngs of paparazzi. As soon as the couple left Scotland, the media firestorm that had been quietly growing really started to burn. While the first engagement rumours were false, Kate's status in the family appeared to grow, as in 2006 she was granted her own security detail through the Royal and Diplomatic Protection Department. William naturally resented the increasing intrusion into his girlfriend's every move – and she was certainly no fan of the constant attention. She was even forced to cancel her participation in a charity boat race in 2007 due to security concerns.

On her 25th birthday, Kate was mobbed by a large throng of paparazzi as she tried to leave for work in the morning. The pressure did nothing for the relationship and Kate made it

> *'Well, I think if you really
> go out with someone for quite
> a long time you do get to know
> each other very, very well.
> You go through the good
> times, you go through the bad
> times. You know, both
> personally, but also within
> a relationship as well.'*
>
> *Kate Middleton*

clear she would not tolerate it. In 2010, she went as far as suing a news agency that distributed pictures of her playing tennis while on holiday, winning damages of £5,000.

Break-Up

By 2007, it appeared the fairy tale was over. Following a holiday together in Zermatt, Switzerland, on 14 April the story broke that the two were no longer a couple, although Clarence House would only say 'we don't comment on Prince William's private life'. The exact reasons for the break-up are not known for sure, but that it was ultimately William's decision is common knowledge. The original report in *The Sun* newspaper quoted a 'close friend' as saying that Middleton felt Prince William had not been paying her enough attention and had been spending time with female friends. It was also said that the Prince, aged 24 at the time, felt he was too young to marry. A report in the *Daily Mail* newspaper blamed a desire by royal courtiers not to 'hurry along' a marriage announcement, and Prince William's desire to enjoy his bachelor status within his army career.

Reunion

The split did not last long. Just two months later, the couple were forced to insist they were 'just good friends' after Middleton attended the 'Concert for Diana' memorial celebration the Princes had organized in honour of their late mother. Kate and William sat two rows apart, but rumours of a reconciliation began to flow nonetheless.

Next, Kate was spotted hunting deer with Prince William at Balmoral, was soon mingling at weddings with him, and supporting him during his RAF wings award ceremony and Order of the Garter presentation. In 2008, Kate even attended the wedding of William's cousin Peter Phillips, while William could not make it. With reports they had decided to give their romance a second chance filling the papers, Kate and William stayed out of the media limelight for as long as possible. They were rarely seen out together at their old haunts. It became obvious that the couple were back together and that the split had only been a short one.

'I think you can get quite consumed by a relationship when you are younger. I really valued that time for me as well, although I didn't think it at the time.'

Kate Middleton on the break-up

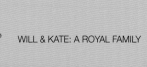

'He did cook for me
at university… always
with a bit of anger if
something went wrong.'

Kate Middleton

> 'She's a fantastic girl,
> she really is. My brother is
> very lucky to have found her
> and she's very lucky to have
> found my brother. I think
> the two of them together
> are a perfect match.'
>
> HRH Prince Harry

Stronger Than Ever

Back together, the couple appeared stronger than ever. In late 2007, Kate had resigned from her job at Jigsaw. Working for her parents' company, Party Pieces, meant she had more time to support the Prince on the sidelines at polo matches, take trips with him and attend all manner of royal events. Kate has admitted she 'wasn't very happy' during their separation, but insists she now sees it as something that made her 'a stronger person'. 'You find out things about yourself that maybe you hadn't realized,' she is quoted as saying.

Engagement

William eventually proposed in 2010, finally putting paid to that 'Waity Katie' moniker. The royal proposal happened on a trip to Kenya. While they elected to keep the exact details of the proposal private, what is known is William picked a quiet moment with his girl on a group trip to pop the question – and according to Kate it was 'very romantic' and a big surprise. In November 2010, Clarence House confirmed that Prince William had proposed to Kate a month earlier, and that the couple were engaged and set to marry. Official photographs were taken, and the couple gave their first interview together, both looking radiantly happy.

Over the years,

William has really looked

after me. He's treated

me very well as the great,

loving boyfriend he is.'

Kate Middleton

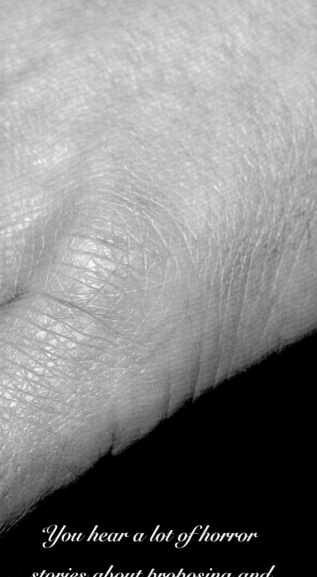

The Ring

William revealed he was paranoid throughout the Kenyan trip, as he had his late mother's engagement ring hidden in his rucksack. He chose to propose to Kate with the sapphire and diamond ring, which obviously held a particularly special meaning. 'It's my mother's engagement ring so I thought it was quite nice because obviously she's not going to be around to share any of the fun and excitement of it all,' William said in the official engagement interview.

'I know inside she is nervous. But it doesn't show, and that's what's important. She looks confident.'

Arthur Edwards, royal photographer

Featuring a 12 carat, oval-cut Ceylon sapphire surrounded by 18 diamonds, set in white gold with a narrow yellow gold band, Kate's engagement ring originally cost £28,500 (in 1981) and its value is now estimated up to £250,000. The ring was one of a selection of eight sent to Diana and Charles by Royal Jeweller Garrard.

'You hear a lot of horror stories about proposing and things going horribly wrong – it went really, really well and I was really pleased when she said yes.'

Prince William on proposing

Wonderful News

News of the royal engagement made headlines around the world, and sparked happy reactions from all corners. The Queen's representatives tweeted: 'The Queen and The Duke of Edinburgh are absolutely delighted at the news of Prince William and Catherine Middleton's engagement.' The monarch and Prince Philip were full of smiles when seen at an official engagement at the University of Sheffield straight after the announcement was made. Enveloped in a media storm, Kate or 'Catherine' as she was suddenly referred to, opted to read to assembled press from a written family statement, read out by father Michael. He and wife Carole said they were 'absolutely delighted' with the news and had, over the years, got to know Will well. 'We all think he's wonderful and we're extremely fond of him. They make a lovely couple, they are great fun to be with and we've had a lot of laughs together.'

Speaking candidly to a television reporter while on an Arctic trek, HRH Prince Harry appeared overjoyed. When asked what his mother would think, he had this to say: 'She'd be very, very proud that the big day has come – you know we all thought it was never going to happen for him, but it has happened and I think everyone's going to be really proud of him and it's a big deal'. 'It's not just a normal wedding, it's a really big decision for him to bring Kate into the family, there's obviously a huge amount of pressure from the media, from the public perception and everything like that. He's done the right thing, he's waited and he's done it when he's felt right.' Clarence House immediately tweeted,

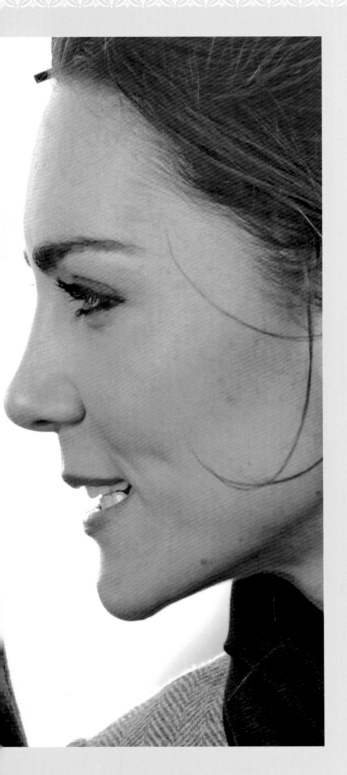

'During a visit to Poundbury in Dorset, The Prince of Wales said he is "thrilled" at the news of Prince William's engagement'. Charles also later joked, 'They've been practising long enough.' His wife Camilla described the engagement as 'the most brilliant news'.

'I thought if I ask Kate first, then [Kate's father] can't really say no, so I did it that way round.'

Prince William

'It's quite good news always to outfox the media. But it was a military style operation and my brother and I are proud of how it went.'

Prince William on his stag do

Wedding Plans

The couple, the Royal Family and British authorities, particularly the Met Police, had much to think about to ensure what was quickly dubbed 'the wedding of the century' went off without a hitch. Much of the cost of the massive celebration would be to do with security. Anti-terrorism and protection measures to protect the Royal Family and visiting world leaders reportedly cost up to £20 million, and included the services of 5,000 armed police in London on the day, as well as snipers on rooftops. The couple themselves were keen to appear budget conscious, however, considering the economic climate. They insisted on canapés only for their main reception, for instance, and drove to the ceremony in cars, rather than the traditional, and far more costly, carriages.

'It's a big deal. It's not just a normal wedding. It's a really big decision for him to bring Kate into the family.'

Prince Harry on Prince William's wedding plans

The Prince enjoyed a stag do, which he managed to keep secret from the media until after the event. Will spent his last weekend as a bachelor at Hartland Abbey in North

Devon, a family mansion of his friend's, where he and a dozen pals even managed a spot of surfing as well as some clay pigeon shooting. Meanwhile, Kate opted to keep things even quieter, celebrating with a 'quiet night in' with a small group of friends.

When and Where

Their courtship was an untraditionally long 10 years, yet once the engagement was revealed, the Royal Family took just seven days to announce a date and location. What was quickly dubbed 'the wedding of the century' was to take place on Friday 29 April 2011 at Westminster Abbey.

The day was swiftly declared a bank holiday so the nation could watch the spectacle and join in the celebrations. According to a royal aide, the couple had pushed for a Friday during spring to wed. BBC News reported they chose the Abbey for 'its staggering beauty, 1000-year royal history and feeling of intimacy despite its size'. Despite its 2,200 capacity, William's private secretary Jamie Lowther-Pinkerton claimed William thought the Abbey felt 'like a parish church'.

The choice of venue came as no surprise, despite its painful association for William – his mother's funeral was also held at Westminster. The only other venue under serious consideration – and unsurprisingly rejected by the young couple – was St Paul's Cathedral, the site where Diana and Charles had wed. The Queen, the Queen Mother, Princess Margaret, Princess Anne and The Duke of York all married at the Abbey.

'William and Kate have thoroughly enjoyed the process of creating their special day. They have been responsible for everything from the smallest detail, such as the reception canapés, to the big decisions like the carriages.'

A Palace spokesman

Doing it Their Way

With only five months until the big day, the young couple had more than enough to keep them occupied. Despite the help of an army of staff, the couple made it clear they would take a hands-on approach when it came to the details.

Kate worked alongside Prince Charles to choose the music. The bride came armed with 'mood boards' when selecting floral arrangements, chose Fiona Cairns to create an eight-tier masterpiece of a wedding cake and was involved in every last wedding detail – even choosing to scent the church with her favourite orange-blossom Jo Malone candles.

William and Kate wanted to make the day as accessible to the public as possible, so wedding coverage was streamed live on YouTube. The Prince's press office also provided a live blog throughout the day.

The couple refused to accept traditional gifts, opting instead for well-wishers to donate to charity. They also went to pains to reassure the public they were aware of the economic climate, insisting on certain less extravagant measures.

You're Not On The List

The highly coveted invitations were sent out by Royal Mail in mid-February. Close to 1,900 people were lucky enough to

receive 'the golden tickets' which, printed on thick white card, were bevelled, gilded and stamped with EIIR in gold, which was then burnished.

While speculation began to mount immediately as to who would make the cut, an official list was not released until 23 April, when Clarence House confirmed it had invited more than 50 members of the Royal Family and 40 crowned heads from Europe and around the world, including the Prince of Saudi Arabia, the King of Tonga, the Sheik of Kuwait and the Princess of Thailand. Over 60 Prime Ministers and governor generals of countries including Australia and New Zealand, Papua New Guinea and Barbados received the invites. William and Kate chose 250 of their friends to attend, while Kate's parents were allowed a quota of 100. Kate's rumoured ex-boyfriends Rupert Finch and Willem Marx, and William's former flames, Isabella Anstruther-Gough-Calthorpe, Arabella Musgrave, Rose Farquhar and Jecca Craig, also received the royal nod. Notable snubs included Barack and Michelle Obama, and Fergie, the Duchess of York as well as William's cousin Beatrice's boyfriend of five years Dave Clark and Lady Annabel Goldsmith, one of Diana's closest friends.

'We're like ducks, all calm on the surface, but the little feet are going under the water.'

Prince William on wedding preparations

'I did the rehearsals the other day and my knees started going, tapping quite nervously, so it's quite a daunting prospect.'

Prince William reveals his nerves with four weeks to go

'It was so great to actually keep a secret, especially in this day and age when everyone talks about everything.'

Dress designer Sarah Burton

The Big Day

The wedding was a triumph, with all going to a very exact plan. By 9.50 am, most of the 1,900 guests were already inside the Abbey for the 11 am service. William and Harry arrived at 10.15 am. The Queen arrived at 10.45 am. Kate was denied the usual bride's indulgence of being late, departing in a Rolls Royce Phantom VI with her father, from the posh Goring Hotel at precisely 10.51 am to get to the Abbey on time.

Public Party

Prime Minister David Cameron had said he wanted the wedding to be 'a day of national celebration' and it certainly was. The British public, not to mention throngs of overseas visitors, embraced the celebratory, flag-waving spirit that swept the nation. Over 5,000 street parties were held to mark the Royal Wedding throughout the UK and one million people lined the route between Westminster Abbey and Buckingham Palace in London. Hardcore royal fans camped out for days to get a good spot. London's Clapham Common was turned into a giant camping ground and crowds gathered to watch big screens in Hyde Park. Over 72 million tuned in to the YouTube Royal Channel. It seemed Royal Wedding mania had swept the land, with even cynics eventually getting caught up in the hype.

You Are On The List

As the congregation arrived, their outfit choices were scrutinized live on TV. Victoria Beckham arrived with hubby David – she in surprisingly towering stilettos, considering her heavily pregnant state; he with O.B.E on the wrong lapel. Both looked fabulous.

Guy Ritchie was there, a distant cousin of Kate's, as were Sir Elton John and David Furnish. William's cousin Princess Beatrice stunned the watching throngs with her strange Philip Treacy hat, which immediately drew myriad comparisons – was she wearing antlers, an octopus or a loo seat? The Queen looked resplendent in yellow, while the PM's wife, Samantha Cameron, raised eyebrows by not wearing a hat.

Get Me To The Church On Time

The ceremony was overseen by John Robert Hall, the Dean of Westminster; Rowan Williams the Archbishop of Canterbury conducted the marriage ceremony itself, while Richard Chartres, the Bishop of London, gave the sermon. Maple trees had been brought into the Abbey giving it a forest-like feel. A reading was given by the bride's brother James.

It was a long, three-and-a-half minute walk down the aisle to the altar. Kate's incredible composure impressed everybody. Prince William looked handsome in the red uniform of his honorary rank of Colonel of the Irish Guards. A memorable

'Poor Posh – she is trying so hard not to smile because she doesn't like her face when she does but she desperately wants to.'

Sports broadcaster Clare Balding on Victoria Beckham

moment occurred when Harry turned to sneak a peek at the bride. 'She's here,' he said to his nervous brother with a grin. 'Just wait till you see her.'

Catherine chose to omit the word 'obey' from her vows, following in Diana's footsteps. She instead promised to 'love, comfort, honour and keep' Prince William. William also broke with royal tradition by having a best man – brother Harry – instead of a 'supporter' as is the norm. Four bridesmaids and two pageboys were led by Pippa Middleton, maid of honour, into the Abbey, followed by Catherine and her father.

The Westminster Abbey Choir, the Chapel Royal Choir – of angelic young male voices – and the London Chamber Orchestra provided much of the music, which had a 'Best of British' theme. Dramatic hymns included 'Greensleeves', 'Jerusalem' and 'Guide Me, O Thou Great Redeemer'. The Central Band of the Royal Air Force provided the fanfare.

'She is so stunningly beautiful, it's so regal, it's such understatement that I think it's just perfection. Everybody is starstruck with her gown.'

Harold Tillman, chair of the British Fashion Council

The Dress

Kate's dress, designed by the late Alexander McQueen's successor Sarah Burton, single-handedly put lace and beading back in bridal fashion. The dress featured a Grace Kelly-inspired lace bodice, hand-stitched by seamstresses from the Royal School of Needlework. The cinched waist emphasized the bride's tiny proportions, while the full skirt and 2.7 m (9 ft) train put paid to speculation Kate would go for

something simple. Fifty-eight gazar buttons ran from the collar to the waist on the gown, which was priced at £250,000.

According to the designer, the gown had 'an essence of Victorian corsetry', with the cinched waist and a bustle to keep the shape of the dress at the back. However, the dress was cut in a modern way and featured intricate handcrafted long, lace sleeves. 'We wanted to look to the past, but look to the future as well,' Burton said.

The media and bookmakers had speculated for months as to who would dress Kate on her wedding day. Preparations were carried out in top secret with seamstresses kept in the dark as to what they were really working on. Pippa Middleton's sleek, sexier, fitted cowl neck maid of honour creation – also by Burton – generated just as much admiration on the day. High street stores scrambled to copy both designs.

Down to the Last Detail

Despite speculation she would wear flowers in her hair, Kate opted to go with a 1936 Cartier 'halo' tiara. It fitted into the 'something borrowed' category, as it was on loan from the Queen herself, who had received it for her 18th birthday. To complement the exquisite tiara, which features 1,000 diamonds, Kate wore a pair of diamond earrings received as a pre-wedding gift from her parents. They featured an acorn design, representing the Middleton family's new coat of arms. Kate's wedding ring is made from Welsh gold, fashioned from a piece the Queen had retrieved from the royal vaults and gifted to William.

'Checkmate Kate –
you've taken the King.'

Words on a banner among the

cheering crowds

'I love where she comes from and who she is. You see them together and they're easy with each other. They look at each other with genuine interest and love. It takes a very special person to step into that world.'

Dame Helen Mirren

Kate's hair was styled in loose curls by James Pryce of Richard Ward Salon. He had spent weeks practising the delicate up-do with a cheap £6.50 imitation tiara. Kate insisted on doing her own make-up, which was typically understated. Her nails were painted in a mixture of two polishes, a 'barely there' pink and 'sheer beige'. The bridal veil was made of soft ivory silk tulle and stitched with flowers. Kate wore size five-and-a-half, hand-stitched, low stiletto, closed-toe shoes.

'I remember standing in Westminster Abbey thinking "this is unreal". It was like a fairy tale. And all I could think was, "I hope I don't trip over". I didn't realise the enormity of it until much nearer the wedding day. It was a magical experience.'

Kate about her wedding day.

The Parade

On leaving the Abbey to the pealing of bells, the couple passed through an individually selected guard of honour made up from defence services, to be greeted by loud cheers from the waiting throngs. According to *Vanity Fair*, as the couple climbed into the Queen's 1902 State Landau carriage, drawn by four white horses, to the pealing of bells, Duchess Catherine turned to her husband and said, 'Are you happy?' 'Very,' he replied, taking her hand. 'This is mad. Gosh, the noise.'

The newly married couple were escorted by mounted escort of the Life Guard on their way back to Buckingham Palace. The weather held, and the crowds continued to cheer. The next big moment was when the bridal party appeared on the balcony of Buckingham Palace. Applause from the crowded Mall was deafening, the crowd cheering, 'kiss, kiss, kiss'. After waving, the couple kissed, ever so briefly, on the lips. William turned to Kate and said: 'Let's give them another one. I love you.' They kissed again and by 1.31 pm it was all over.

Just Married

As guests thronged in the courtyard of the palace, another break from tradition was about to occur. William hopped in to the driver's seat of his dad's Aston Martin DB6 Volante. The car had been a 21st birthday present from Queen Elizabeth to her son. William drove his new bride the short distance to the London home of Charles and Camilla, Clarence House.

'William spoke very well, but it was Charles who really gave praise to his daughter-in-law. He said they were really lucky to have a daughter like her.'

Dr Robert Acheson, the headmaster of Kate's former primary school

Prince Harry had decorated the Aston Martin with a number plate, JU5T WED. The couple were accompanied by a bright yellow RAF search and rescue chopper.

Private Parties

The wedding became more intimate and exclusive as the day wore on. A lunchtime reception at Buckingham Palace hosted by the Queen saw 650 invited. A team of 21 chefs prepared 'finger food' fare the couple had requested, featuring mini Yorkshire puddings with beef, Cornish crab salad and Scottish smoked salmon.

By 7 pm, the Queen had departed and the next party, with just 300 guests, had begun, guests arriving in blacked-out limos. Kate changed into a strapless white McQueen evening gown, with diamanté sash. Just before midnight, guests were led into the Throne Room, transformed into a nightclub. The bride and groom took to the floor to a rendition of Elton John's 'Your Song' by Ellie Goulding, whom they had specially requested for the evening. A fireworks display ended the night with a bang at 2.30 am.

The Honeymoon

The couple waited ten days before setting off on their honeymoon, flying to a private island in the Seychelles, where they had previously stayed in 2007 on a 'make or break' trip. They flew by private jet from Anglesey to a luxury villa with its own pool and butler service.

Married Life

The newlyweds were quick to settle into a 'normal' routine on the island of Anglesey, just off the coast of north-west Wales. During the post-wedding, pre-honeymoon days Kate was photographed pushing a trolley at the local Waitrose, while William showed up on Monday morning following the Friday ceremony for a normal shift of work as an RAF search and rescue pilot. New wife Kate refused the extra household staff offered and instead insisted on doing all the cooking for William herself - including his favourite, roast chicken.

The low-key royals adored the peace and relative privacy remote Anglesey offers. They savoured many a long walk together on the island's near-deserted beaches and were warmly welcomed into the community. On his jogs through the village, the Duke was known to wave to passing locals, meanwhile the couple became regulars at The White Eagle pub, where William enjoyed the odd pint of bitter; the Duchess sticking to white wine or sparkling water.

Anglesey Abode

Surrounded by private land in the south west of Anglesey and breathtakingly positioned above the Irish Sea, William and Kate's first home – a four-bedroom, whitewashed farmhouse located in the Welsh-speaking hamlet of Bodorgan – was rented by William from royal confidant Sir George Meyrick for £750 per

month. With a private beach accessible only by foot and a race track William loved to ride his Ducati around, the property became a welcome, treasured sanctuary for the famous royal couple and later, for baby George, too. The Cambridges were guarded by a seven-strong royal protection team housed in converted outbuildings. The exact location and layout of the family's first home was only revealed once they had moved. The royal presence had a positive effect on local tourism, boosting visitor numbers by an estimated 140,000 per year.

'I have never in my life known somewhere as beautiful and as welcoming as Anglesey... I know that both of us will miss it terribly.'

Prince William speaking at the Anglesey Show.

William publicly expressed regret at having to leave Anglesey, as his time with RAF Valley reached its conclusion. 'This island had been our first home together, and it will always be an immensely special place for us both,' he told locals at the Anglesey Show on 15 August 2013. 'Catherine and I look forward to returning again and again over the coming years with our family.' During his three years with RAF Valley, William – known as Flight Lieutenant Wales – took part in 156 search and rescue operations, with 149 people being rescued.

'I'm just very grateful to Kate Middleton for making looking appropriate really fun again.'

Anne Hathaway

'No one is going to try to fill my mother's shoes, what she did was fantastic. It's about making your own future and your own destiny and Kate will do a very good job of that.'

Prince William

Moving On

November 2011 saw the public informed of the Duke and Duchess's intention to make Apartment 1A, Kensington Palace – the late Princess Margaret's apartment – their permanent family home. Before the Cambridges could even think about moving in, extensive renovations had to be completed. Empty since the Queen's sister died in 2002, much of the apartment had remained painted in Princess Margaret's favourite colours: turquoise and pink. Kate put in many hours to ensure the residence was redecorated to her and William's tastes. In September 2013, having left Wales, the couple, along with George and family cocker spaniel Lupo, finally settled themselves into their new 21-room residence. Far grander than their Anglesey place, 1A has four floors, a large dining room, drawing room, study, nursery and walled garden.

Kensington Palace remains the Cambridge family's 'official' residence. However, it's widely known that Wills and Kate prefer life in the countryside. So, they're expected to continue making the most of Anmer Hall, the country retreat gifted to them by the Queen. The Grade 2 listed, ten-bedroom Georgian property has a swimming pool and tennis court and is two miles from the Queen's Sandringham Estate in Norfolk. It's also handy for Cambridge Airport, where William's new job as an air ambulance pilot sees him based. Renovations at Anmer in preparation for their arrival personally cost Wills and Kate £1.5 million and took a full two years to complete. A new kitchen, driveway, and extensive planting for privacy were among some of the modifications.

Royal Tours

In June, 2011, Kate and Wills departed on their first ever official overseas trip, to North America. All eyes were on Kate and she didn't disappoint, conducting herself with poise and appearing happy and confident. It was Kate's first time to the States, and she and Wills mingled with Barack and Michelle Obama and Hollywood stars. September 2012 was a repeat stellar performance as the Duke and Duchess embarked on a nine-day tour of the Far East to celebrate the Queen's Diamond Jubilee. The royal tours were interrupted by the birth of Prince George, who was born in St Mary's Hospital in London on the morning of 22nd July 2013. The couple's third royal tour, a three-week stint in Australasia in April 2014 was extra special, as it was also baby Prince George's first overseas trip. The tot completely stole the show. Of course.

'He's growing quite quickly actually. But he's a little fighter – he wriggles around quite a lot and he doesn't want to go to sleep that much.'

William on baby George

Queen of Style

With her tiny waistline, lustrous blow-dry, radiant complexion and ability to pull off striking colour choices including white and scarlet, Kate's evolving, elegant style is admired across the globe. The Duchess, who loves cinched waistlines, modest hemlines, dainty jewellery and fascinators, regularly features on 'best dressed' lists. Although she has not been without critics. In 2011, Dame Vivienne Westwood said: 'I would have loved to dress Kate Middleton but I'll have to wait until she kind of catches up a bit with style.' At New York Fashion Week the same year, the local 'fash pack' said Kate followed trends rather than set them.

'I'm shaking – she's not just one of those pretty people in magazines. She's actually even prettier.'

Fan Chiara Guglielmi, on meeting Kate in Canada

Becoming An Icon

Since then, Kate's fashion choices have been working hard to silence critics. She's also become an expert when it comes to pulling off maternity-wear-chic. The Duchess had the fashion crowd talking – in an admiring way – when she donned a stunning pale jade crepe Jenny Packham gown with thigh high underskirt to the Natural History Museum in October 2014, while approximately 14 weeks pregnant. She also dazzled in a cut-out Temperley frock at another charity event held the same week, a risqué choice for the Duchess, but one she pulled off with ease. Her gradually more daring style choices show Kate is relaxing into her role as fashion icon and having more fun with her outfits.

Entire websites are dedicated to following Kate's every fashion move. She first began attracting attention in fashion pages in 2006, when *The Daily Telegraph* named her Most Promising Newcomer in its list of style winners and losers. *Tatler* ranked her among 10 style icons in 2007, and since then she has been lauded by a myriad of publications, from *Vanity Fair* to *Vogue*, from Style.com to *People*. In 2011, *Harper's Bazaar* named the Duchess 'Britain's Queen of Style' at its Women of the Year Awards. Early in 2015 it was revealed *Vogue* editor Anna Wintour was trying to get Kate to appear on its September cover.

The Kate Effect

In what has been dubbed 'The Kate Effect', any item of clothing the Duchess is pictured in quickly sells out. After Kate chose a navy blue, long sleeve Issa design for her engagement announcement, stocks of the £385 dress sold out within a day. The £595 cut-out Emblem Flare Dress by Temperley Kate wore to an Action on Addiction gala dinner in October 2014 sold out within hours, meanwhile stocks of a £700 Goat frock she wore the next month were snapped up in minutes.

Kate is a champion of British fashion. Her choices regularly make a patriotic statement while helping to boost sales. Home-grown labels she favours include Reiss, Burberry, Temperley, Mulberry and Amanda Wakeley, whose couture was also loved by Diana, Princess of Wales. British designers

Katherine Hooker, Jenny Packham and Sophie Cranston of Libelula have also benefited from Kate's patronage. The Duchess's favourite maternity labels are Seraphine and Madderson London. Incredibly, the see-through £30 dress that famously caught William's eye in 2002 sold at auction for $125,871 in 2011.

'She's modern, really modern. She's smart to mix cheap clothes with the likes of Alexander McQueen.'

Anna Dello Russo, editor-at-large of VOGUE *Japan*

Royal Recycler

Kate has no qualms about recycling her outfits, or mixing her designer wear with bargains from the high street. For instance, on 19 February 2015, while heavily pregnant, she wore a lovely flowered number from Seraphine to the Cape Hill Children's Centre – exactly the same dress she'd debuted a month earlier whilst visiting family friends in Kensington. The white Zara blouse she wore to her first public outing following

the birth of baby George was the same one she was pictured in while five months pregnant. She often sports a pair of blue Jimmy Choo heels, which she bravely continued to wear throughout her second pregnancy, even at seven months.

Pre-honeymoon, she was famously photographed on the King's Road in London selecting outfits from Whistles, Banana Republic and Warehouse. Kate also loves Zara, French Connection and LK Bennett. She wore a Top Shop dress at her 25th birthday bash, and another to visit Warner Brothers Studios whilst heavily pregnant with George. Despite her love of the high street, Kate can glam it up with the best of them, as she did in the Diane Von Furstenberg number she chose for the Royal Variety Performance in November 2014.

> *'I haven't given her any style advice. Why would she need any from me? She never puts a foot wrong. She knows what suits her.'*
>
> *Style guru and Kate's step-sister-in-law Sara Buys, wife of Tom Parker Bowles*

The George Effect

Even before he turned one, baby George had already earned his fashion stripes. From the gown worn at his christening – a replica of one used for Queen Victoria's eldest daughter in 1841 – George's outfits have been keenly followed in the media, and just as keenly copied by parents worldwide. Versions of the items he wore on his debut Australasian tour in 2014 were quickly snapped up, meanwhile the boy singlehandedly spawned mini-trends for tots, popularizing cardigan sweaters, safari-style shorts, striped overalls and nautical-themed wear. *Vogue* named the Prince the world's most photographed infant on a list of 2014's most stylish children while he was ranked 49th on *GQ*'s 50 Best Dressed Men in Britain list in 2015. Not bad, considering he's still just a tot!

> *'Parents across the country are seeking inspiration from the royals in how their little ones look. Like his mum, Prince George has proved to be a trendsetter.'*
>
> *Camilla Rowe, children's wear buyer, John Lewis*

Parenthood

On 3 December 2012, St James's Palace announced that the Duke and Duchess of Cambridge were expecting their first baby. The news was made public early, as Kate had severe morning sickness. She was admitted into hospital the same day to receive hydration and nutrients. it was not known how long the couple had known about the pregnancy but the Queen only found out earlier the same day as the public.

Kate recovered well, and took part in public engagements right up until 15 June 2013, when she looked radiant in a pink Alexander McQueen ensemble at the Trooping of the Colour parade. Leading up to the birth, she kept fit via swimming and pre-natal yoga classes. In January 2013 succession laws were changed, meaning a girl baby would have equal right to the throne.

It's A Boy!

On the morning of 22 July 2013, the Duchess was admitted to the Lindo wing of St Mary's Hospital, the same hospital and wing in which Diana gave birth to William and Harry. At 16.24, after ten hours of labour, Kate gave birth – by natural delivery – to a baby boy weighing 8 lbs 6 oz. William was by his wife's side. The couple had chosen not to find out the sex of the baby prior to the birth and so were in for a surprise, as were the throngs of photographers and well wishers camped outside the hospital and indeed the whole world, which had been waiting with bated breath for this most anticipated birth.

George Alexander Louis

Kate was allowed to return home the next day. As she, William and their new arrival emerged onto the hospital steps, the baby wrapped up in a white shawl, they were greeted by cheering and camera clicks. William joked with a reporter that 'thankfully' the child had his mother's looks. 'He's got a good pair of lungs on him, that's for sure,' he said. Kate said she felt 'very emotional' following the birth and revealed that Wills changed the Prince's first nappy. 'He's very good at it,' she claimed. The following day the delighted parents announced they had named their boy George Alexander Louis – official title His Royal Highness Prince George of Cambridge. Following his grandfather and father, George is third in line to the throne.

First Royal Events

Prince George has been keenly photographed and cooed over wherever he goes. On 23 October 2013, George was christened by the Archbishop of Canterbury in the Chapel Royal at St James's Palace. The Duke and Duchess chose to elect eight godparents.

April 2014 saw the little Prince embark on his first royal tour, to Australasia, during which he made two official appearances. The first was a play date with other ten other tots in Wellington, New Zealand. George crawled around with confidence and was well received, although he made a little

'It's such a special time. I think any parent will know what this feeling feels like.'

Kate, immediately after George's birth

> *'He's a little bit of a rascal, I'll put it that way. He either reminds me of my brother or me when I was younger.'*
>
> *William on George*

girl cry when he took her wooden toy, prompting one guest to describe him as 'a little bruiser'. His second public appearance saw him meet a bilby named after him at Taronga Zoo, Sydney. George squealed with delight when he saw the rat-like marsupial. As the keeper made to coax the bilby closer, Kate stepped in to stop him, saying 'He's got quite a strong grab, actually.' Following the tour, the BBC noted there was 'no doubt Prince George stole the limelight'.

All About George

George's parents have said he loves painting and swimming, sweet potatoes and opening and closing doors. He also loves wombats, a fact revealed when the Prince was given a wombat book. 'He's really into them,' Kate said. She also confessed he was 'very, very loud' telling a young Australian well-wisher she was worried he would scare the animals at Taronga Zoo!

On 22 July 2014 Prince George celebrated his first birthday. The party was themed around Peter Rabbit by Beatrix Potter, an author related to George's maternal ancestors. The Queen was in attendance, as were Prince Harry, Zara and Mike Tindall and the Middletons. For George's big day, the Royal Mint celebrated by striking 7,500 sterling silver coins. The photographer who took the official pictures described him as 'quick on his feet'.

Welcoming
Charlotte Elizabeth Diana

On 8 September 2014, Clarence House announced Kate was pregnant again. The news was delivered earlier than expected – for the second time – due to Kate's extreme morning sickness, which saw her cancel public engagements. Following a pregnancy during which she was once again admired for her elegance and poise, on 2nd May 2015 Kate gave birth to a baby girl weighing 8 lbs 3 oz. The new addition was welcomed warmly into the Cambridge clan and is fourth in line to the throne.

'Suddenly you start thinking, wow, there is stuff you want to safeguard for the future. I've always believed it, but to actually really feel it as well, it's coming through powerfully now.'

William on the effect George's birth had on his charity work

What Lies Ahead

Following the expiration of his RAF contract in 2013, the Duke enjoyed, for a year, what his office termed a 'period of transition,' while he considered carefully what to do next. A position within the Foreign Office was considered and dismissed, as were various private sector roles. In August 2014, it was announced that William's next career move would see him become an air ambulance pilot for the East Anglian Air Ambulance, a charitable organisation that relies solely on private fundraising and donations.

All For Charity

Wills indicated he was looking forward to beginning operations in the summer of 2015, giving him some free time to focus on his family following the birth of newest addition, Charlotte. The Duke has said he will donate his £40,000 salary to charity. He has committed himself to the role for at least two years, doing both day and night shifts based out of Cambridge Airport, which is within 50 miles of his and Kate's Anmer Hall residence.

When not at work, the Duke will continue to keep busy aiding various charities, including United For Wildlife, which has brought together seven of the most influential conservation bodies to work with his Royal Foundation against the poaching of animals. Following the birth of their son George, William said his charity work had taken on a new purpose as he thought of 'the world that dear George would inherit'.

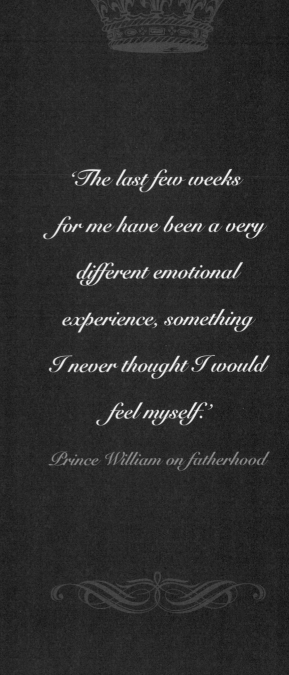

'The last few weeks for me have been a very different emotional experience, something I never thought I would feel myself.'

Prince William on fatherhood

Royal Association

Aiding charities is a big part of being a modern Royal, and William is not the only one with causes to champion. Soon after they were married, he and Kate personally selected 26 charitable organizations that had 'particular resonance' with them to benefit from their wedding fund. These included the London Zoo's black rhino project and Beatbullying; the latter is thought to have been included due to Kate's personal experience of being bullied at school.

Together with Prince Harry, Kate and Wills established The Royal Foundation in 2011. The Foundation has three main areas of focus: supporting the Armed Forces, conservation

and young people. Charities Kate has personally aligned herself with include Action on Addiction and SportsAid and the Scout Association. She even volunteered as an assistant leader while on Anglesey.

Happy Families

One day, they will become King and Queen of England. (If Kate becomes Queen, she will be the first queen of the United Kingdom to hold a university degree.) Until then, the Duke and Duchess of Cambridge will be expected to keep up a steady stream of public appearances and overseas tours, maintain their charity work and of course, take care of their young children.

Thankfully, William and Kate appear by all accounts to be the perfect, happily married couple. Their children are contented and healthy and get to enjoy the hands-on parenting style favoured by the modern royals. As the Royal Family's golden couple, there is a lot of genuine public affection for Kate and Wills. They will, at all costs, want to avoid scandal and divorce.

'[Our son] has Catherine's looks, thankfully.'

Prince William

Biographies

Alice Hudson (Author)

From New Zealand, **Alice Hudson** fused twin passions for writing and music while a student, reviewing and interviewing international bands and DJs. She is currently based in London, writing and researching for corporate clients across a wide range of sectors, from health and fitness and financial services, to social media and entertainment.

Joe Little (Foreword)

Joe Little has been managing editor of *Majesty* for 12 years. In that time he has met some weird and wonderful people, and has travelled extensively on royal assignments. Highlights include a fantastic trip to Kuala Lumpur, where he found himself dancing the *poco-poco* with the Queen of Malaysia, and a long weekend in Riyadh, flying on one of the King of Saudi Arabia's private aircraft. Joe's working life is almost as varied as that of Queen Elizabeth II and her family, and occasionally he gets to meet them too.

Picture Credits

Image © Tim Rooke/Rex Shutterstock: 119. Images © Getty Images: Samir Hussein 4, 7, 25, 53, 54, 68, 90, 92, 124; Chris Jackson 8, 14, 50, 53, 56, 58, 59, 64, 66, 80, 112; Antony Jones/Julian Parker/Mark Cuthbert 10; John Stillwell/AFP 12, 120, 124; Ken Goff/Time Life Pictures 17; Tim Graham 18, 21, 26, 32; Frazer Harrison/Getty Images for British Consul-General-Los Angeles 20, 24;Scott Barbour 22; Indigo 29, 44, 49, 88, 109; WPA Pool 30, 74, 78, 82, 94, 97, 103, 110, 111; Max Mumby/Indigo 31, 98, 100, 106, 107, 122, 128; Middleton Family/Clarence House via GettyImages 34, 35; Anwar Hussein Collection/ROTA/WireImage 36, 86; Mark Large/Pool 38; Bruno Vincent 39; Stringer/AFP 40; Sang Tan/AFP 42; Mark Allan/WireImage 46; Paul Ellis/AFP 60; Andrew Milligan/WPA Pool 62; Adrian Dennis/AFP 71; Dan Kitwood 72, 76; Fiona Hanson/WPA Pool 77, 73; Peter Macdiarmid 84; Ben Pruchnie/Stringer 104; Mark Cuthbert 105; Neil Mockford/Alex Huckle/Stringer 108; Handout 112, 117; Saeed Khan 114; Danny Martindale 126.